To My Son, With Love

A MOTHER'S MEMORY BOOK

Written and Illustrated by
DONNA GREEN

To My Son, With Love by Donna Green (1952-   )
First published in 2003 by Vermilion Inc.

This edition published in 2007 by
MOON LADY PRESS, Inc.

P.O. Box 83, Marshfield, Hills Ma. 02051, USA

For more information about the art of Donna Green write to:
The Donna Green Studio PO. Box 83, Marshfield Hills Ma. 02051 USA
Or contact her website:
http://www.donnagreen.com

Editor: Robert Fremont,
Editorial/Art Assistant Adam Parent
Design by Carol Belanger Grafton
Assistant designer: Donna Green
Text typeset by CBG Graphics
Photography Gamma One Conversions

Composition:Trufont Typographers, Inc.

ISBN: 978-0-9753473-2-4
Standard Edition

Printed and bound in Singapore by Imago Publishing, Ltd.
5th printing

For my Dad,
who encouraged me to paint

For Bob,
who never stopped believing in me

and

for my son, Adam,
my inspiration

Contents

ABOUT MY SON

My little Son, who look'd from thoughtful eyes
And moved and spoke in quiet grown-up wise.
—COVENTRY PATMORE

To My Son

This is a journal about you and me, mother and son. It's my gift to you. It may be the most precious gift I will ever be able to give you. It's filled with love and important recollections of a lifetime to help you to understand who I am and why you have become the special person you are. It is my hope that you will enjoy reading this book from time to time whenever you'd like to reminisce. Each event I've written about, every feeling, is a piece in the intricate mosaic of our relationship. I don't know why some memories shine like bright pennies and others dim and disappear, but they do. It's the bright shiny pennies of our life together that I've written about.

With love,

About Our Family

*F*amily roots stretch in so many directions that it's sometimes difficult to remember where they all began. High Wampanoag cheekbones accompanied by flaming red hair and too many freckles seem to be a well-loved recipe in our family. The insatiable love for art and music passed down from an eccentric grandfather also repeats itself over a few generations. Whatever the glorious combination, every family has its own unique flavor. This is your family potpourri:

Your grandparents . . .

_____

_____

Our interesting ancestors . . .

_____

_____

_____

_____

Family traits that have been passed down to you . . .

_____

_____

_____

_____

Those Before Us

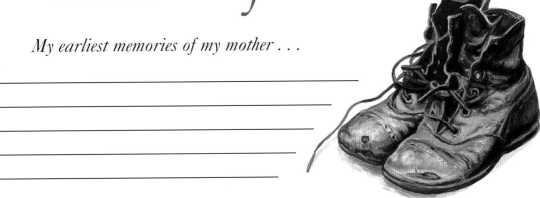

My earliest memories of my mother . . .

_____

_____

_____

_____

_____

My earliest memories of my father . . .

_____

_____

_____

_____

The oldest photograph I love of

_____

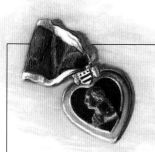

Reflections

Heartaches and struggles . . .

_____

_____

_____

Extraordinary events survived and overcome . . .

_____

_____

_____

Beliefs and military history . . .

_____

_____

      _____

      _____

      _____

      _____

O' blessed vision! Happy child
Thou art so exquisitely wild
I think of thee with many fears
For what may be thy lot
In future years.

—WILLIAM WORDSWORTH

I Remember

Family traditions . . .

_____

_____

_____

Funny things that happened in our family . . .

_____

_____

_____

Places our family thought of as sacred or special . . .

_____

_____

_____

Home is not where you live, but where they understand you.
—CHRISTIAN MORGENSTERN

11

The Good Old Days

A close friend of mine recently showed me an old photograph of himself as a child. His father had taken it of him as he stood fishing with his dog. Underneath the photo in very confident-looking script was the caption his father had given the picture . . . "Presidential Material."

Things unique about our family . . .

_____

_____

_____

_____

Fond memories of the past . . .

_____

_____

_____

_____

Advice passed on . . .

_____

_____

_____

_____

If my father's child can get to be president,
your father's child can make his heart's desire.
—ABRAHAM LINCOLN

Once Upon A Time

My regrets about the past . . .

_____

_____

_____

_____

Old family secrets . . .

_____

_____

_____

_____

Unique lifestyles in our family . . .

_____

_____

_____

_____

Favorite Things and Lifestyles

Interesting family occupations . . .

_____

_____

_____

Special talents and achievements . . .

_____

_____

_____

Cherished heirlooms passed down . . .

_____

_____

_____

The farther back you can look, the farther forward you are likely to see.
—WINSTON CHURCHILL

Love and Marriage

My grandparents were like salt and pepper; one never very far from the other. They communicated with their eyes. Granddad had a twinkle and Grandma knew how to keep it there. One of my fondest memories is seeing them walking hand in hand out to the garden one morning. He stopped and, while opening the gate for her, gently kissed her hand, looking into that sweet face he'd grown old with. I believe he never loved her more than at that moment.

The most special marriage in our family . . .

_____

_____

_____

What made it work so well and for so long . . .

_____

_____

_____

_____

The art of being wise is the art of knowing what to overlook.

—WILLIAM JAMES

How do I love thee? Let me count the ways.
I love thee to the depth and breadth and height
My soul can reach, when feeling out of sight
For the ends of Being and ideal Grace.
I love thee to the level of everyday's
Most quiet need, by sun and candle-light.
I love thee freely, as men strive for Right;
I love thee purely, as they turn from Praise.
I love thee with the passion put to use
In my old griefs, and with my childhood's faith.
I love thee with a love I seemed to lose
With my lost saints,—I love thee with the breath,
Smiles, tears, of all my life!—and, if God choose,
I shall but love thee better after death.

—ELIZABETH BARRETT BROWNING

Grandpa's Wisdom

I'll never forget the day my dad took my son Adam fishing for the first time. He painstakingly tied a rope around his waist to keep him from falling off the pier and then patiently showed him how to bait his hook. What he wasn't aware of was that, while he was demonstrating how to fish, Adam was more interested in putting a worm in his coffee cup. He was so pleased that his grandson was enjoying the fishing as he watched him sitting there with that big grin on his face . . . waiting . . . ever . . . so . . . patiently . . .

What I learned from my dad . . .

_____

_____

_____

_____

Words that still ring in my ears . . .

_____

_____

_____

_____

Advice given and appreciated . . .

_____

_____

_____

_____

*There is a wonderful, mystical law of nature that the three things we
crave most in life . . . happiness, freedom, and peace of mind . . .
are always attained by giving them to someone else.* —ANON

About Myself

Perhaps I should start by telling you that who I have become is largely due to having you in my life. In all my years of trying to decide what I would be and where I would go, everything fell into place during those first few moments that I held you. I instantly wanted to be the best mom I could possibly be. In knowing this, the other decisions were simple. Whatever I set out to accomplish would be with fortitude and passion, always believing in myself, the way I wanted you to go after your dreams. I was forced to look at my own life through your eyes, hopefully making the best decisions for both of us. You and I seem to be growing up and learning about life together! If there is one thing I would like you to know about me, it's that I want my life to matter. I want to leave this world a little bit better than when I entered it. I feel confident that I've already accomplished this by having you!

The Day I Was Born

In our life there is a single color,
As on an artist's palette,
Which provides the meaning of life and art.
It is the color of love. —MARC CHAGALL

_____

The name I was given at birth

_____

Where I was born

PLACE
FOR
PHOTO

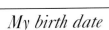
My birth date

My age when you
were born

My favorite childhood photograph of myself

It goes without saying, that you should never have more children than you have car windows. —ERMA BOMBECK

When I Was Young

Isn't it funny how some things never change? My mom would no sooner have the words off her lips asking who wanted to go to the general store before my brother and I would fly to the station wagon with our life and death mission to capture the front seat. "I call 'shot gun,'" he'd scream as my long gangly legs passed him at the gate. "You had it last time," I'd squeal in the most irritating pitch I could manage. Meanwhile, my younger brother and sister would start the "he's looking at me" routine in the rear seat. "All this for a loaf of bread?" Mom would ask as she turned the key.

My warmest memories of those years . . .

_____

_____

_____

_____

The story most often told about me . . .

_____

_____

_____

_____

My most embarrassing moment as a child . . .

_____

_____

_____

_____

My Home Town

"I'm going downtown," I'd yell as I flew out the door grabbing a wagon full of bottles to buy penny candy. In those days, my mom was always there when we got home from school. The neighborhood kids were like family. We'd play hopscotch in the street, kickball and red rover in the field until dusk then switch to hide-and-seek until Dad called us to wash up for dinner. The smell of warm bread greeted us as we all sat down together as a family. I often wish I could slow the world down a bit to those days when our greatest concern was whether or not we'd hear the ice cream truck passing by our house.

My memories of home . . .

_____

_____

_____

The best things to do there . . .

_____

_____

_____

Where we worshipped . . .

_____

_____

School Days

When I first started school, my mom made three new dresses for me to wear. I can still remember every detail that she put into them. On the first day I wore the red one with the yellow bric-a-brac. On the second day I wore the blue one. On the third day I wore the yellow one with red bric-a-brac. And on the fourth day I refused to go to school anymore!

My first school

_____

My favorite teacher

_____

My earliest school memory . . .

_____

_____

_____

_____

I remember getting in trouble when I . . .

_____

_____

_____

After School

I think that I learned more by hanging upside-down in trees every afternoon than I ever did in school. My imagination took me to places never mentioned in text books. I learned strategic thinking, diplomacy and motivation while engaging in intense chestnut wars with the boys next door. Compassion and a sense of pride were learned at the side of an aging woman who I helped with daily chores. Faith, morality and direction were lessons carried the furthest; these a gift from a very wise earth angel who took me under her wing and taught me how to fly.

My warmest childhood memory . . .

_____

_____

_____

What I did after school . . .

_____

_____

_____

My best friend . . .

_____

What I did in those days that might surprise you . . .

_____

_____

_____

My mother wanted me to be her wings to fly as she never quite had the courage to do. I love her for that. I love that she wanted to give birth to her own wings.

—ERICA JONG

Some men see things as they are and ask why. Others dream things that never were and say why not?
—GEORGE BERNARD SHAW

Daydreams

Every day after school the first thing I did was grab my baseball glove and head for the field behind our house. The boys next door would do the same. I reveled in the idea that I was not a wimpy girl. In fact, I could slug a baseball farther than any boy on that field. Then one day, one of the boys helped me up when I skinned my knee on third base. He started to hit the ball better than me too. For some reason I didn't mind.

The best scheme I ever hatched . . .

_____

_____

_____

My dreams about growing up . . .

_____

_____

_____

My favorite place to hide . . .

_____

_____

_____

Your children are not your children.
They are the sons and daughters of life's
longing for itself. You may house their
bodies but not their souls, for their souls
dwell in the house of tomorrow, which you
cannot visit, not even in your dream.

—KAHLIL GIBRAN

In My Room

My room was my cocoon, a place to hide and feel safe. I disguised Mom's pretty wallpaper with dried corsages, torn ticket stubs, and posters. The sensitive butterfly within me took flight on the wings of my music. John Lennon's "Imagine," Joni's lingering lyrics, or the Moody Blues, dancing on the edge of magic, became my understanding world. Being a teenager is such a thorny time. It seems as though the need for freedom and the feeling of vulnerability go hand in hand.

What my room looked like . . .

_____

_____

_____

The view from my window . . .

_____

_____

_____

I loved collecting . . .

_____

_____

_____

Dear Diary

My deepest, darkest secret . . .

_____
_____
_____
_____

What I did that would have surprised my parents . . .

_____
_____
_____
_____

My most daring adventure . . .

_____
_____
_____
_____

My friends . . .

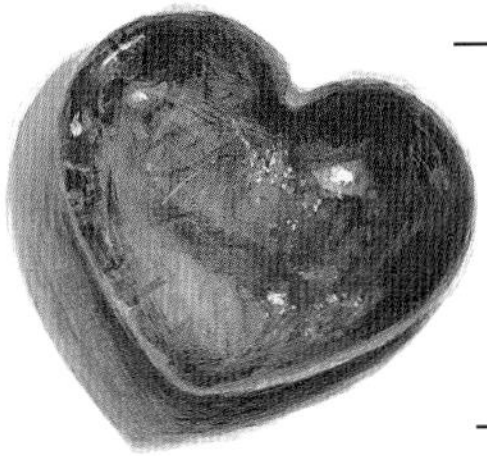

_____
_____
_____
_____

*Within me burned the heart of Amelia, flying
fearlessly from one rainbow's end to the next,
forever longing for encouragement or bravery
to set me free. Then one day . . . I dared to believe.
The view is breathtaking!*
—DONNA GREEN

Boys

I was five and Stevie was six. We were a match made in the land of chocolate milk and Crayolas. He had the brownest eyes and the sweetest smile. I loved sharing secret adventures with him. Oh how my heart broke the day Cindy White swept him away with her pet turtle!

The first boy who noticed me back . . .

_____

My first real love . . .

_____

What I learned that I'd like you to know . . .

_____

_____

_____

Love in your heart is not put there to stay.
Love isn't love till you give it away.
—OSCAR HAMMERSTEIN II

Sometimes It's the Little Things

My dad was either a saint or insane to volunteer to teach me how to drive! As I got into the car and adjusted the mirror to see if my face looked okay, Dad smiled at me patiently and said, "Put it in reverse and let's go!" An hour and a half later, after going down a one-way street the wrong way and getting distracted by a ladybug crawling across the dashboard as I drove through a red light, Dad calmly announced that he felt a little tired and thought it might be a good time to go home.

My first car

_____

My first job

_____

_____

The person who taught me to drive

_____

The best place I ever went . . .

_____

_____

My most important birthday . . .

_____

_____

The most meaningful award I ever received . . .

_____

_____

The whole secret of life is to be interested in one thing
profoundly and a thousand other things well.

—HUGH WALPOLE

My Passions

As I look back on my childhood, I realize that the passionate way I lived as a young girl is exactly where I want to be as an adult. I've come all this way only to realize that holding onto happiness is remembering how to let go.

MY FAVORITE

Pastime

_____

Music

_____

Book

_____

Sport

_____

Season

_____

Food

_____

Reaching for Dreams

Hold fast to dreams
For if dreams die
Life is a broken-winged bird that cannot fly.

Hold fast to dreams
For when dreams go,
Life is a barren field frozen with snow.

—LANGSTON HUGHS

What I dreamed about as a child . . .

_____
_____
_____
_____
_____
_____

What I dream will be
yours someday . . .

_____
_____
_____
_____
_____
_____
_____
_____

Love Makes Us Real

For a long time, each day blended into the next, like rain falling into an ever expanding puddle. Then one day, everything felt different. The sun came out, my heart smiled, and all was right with the world. When love is meant to be, it feels as though your soul has a beautiful garden in which to gently grow old. My son, when you find this, cherish and nurture it with all that you hold sacred for it is truly a gift from God.

How I met your dad . . .

_____

_____

What I found most interesting about him . . .

_____

_____

How you remind me of him . . .

_____

_____

His greatest talents . . .

_____

_____

Love starts when another person's needs become more important than your own. —ANON

Your Dad and I

How your dad and I are alike . . .

_____
_____
_____
_____
_____

How your dad and I are different . . .

_____
_____
_____
_____

My dreams for him . . .

_____
_____
_____

It's such a powerful connection; it takes me by surprise.
I feel like there's a dotted line connecting me to my son.

—SARAH LANGSTON

Then There Was You

There is no way to describe the completeness a woman feels when she first learns that another heart beats beneath her own or that she is about to adopt a child. I felt so blessed—in awe of nature. It didn't seem possible that in just a few short weeks a new little being would be in my arms.

The name you were given at birth

_____

Time of birth

_____

My favorite baby photo of you

PLACE
FOR
PHOTO

Your birth date

_____

Your birth place

_____

I remember leaving the hospital thinking, "Wait, are they going to let me just walk off with him? I don't know beans about babies! I don't have a license to do this."

—ANNE TYLER

About My Son

*I*t was as if time stood still the day you arrived. Birds sounded more beautiful, delicate baby scents floated in the air, and everything finally fell into place. I was so proud of my new son.

Your father's first words . . .

_____

Whom you resembled . . .

_____

_____

My memories of the day you were born . . .

_____

_____

_____

_____

The feelings I experienced that moment I first held you . . .

_____

_____

_____

_____

*There is an enduring tenderness in the
love of a mother to a son that transcends
all other affections of the heart.*

—WASHINGTON IRVING

The Toddler Years

Why is it that children rarely want to get into the bath tub, and yet, when their fingers and toes are all puckered from an hour in the murky sea, they want no part of getting out!? AND . . . why do I think that someday I'll miss that squishy bar of soap and the twenty-two army men clogging the drain?

Where we lived . . .

_____

_____

_____

Little ways you made me smile . . .

_____

_____

_____

Your humorous expressions . . .

_____

_____

_____

_____

_____

Your favorite toy . . .

_____

_____

_____

_____

_____

When You Were a Little Boy

When my son was small he had an amazing talent for finding "neat" stuff to hide in his pockets. Bubble gum, bottle caps, grass, rocks . . . whatever caught his interest was instantly tucked away for later. One laundry day, while doing my usual pocket clean-out, I reached in and pulled out a very squished caterpillar.

I wonder if he remembers the deal we made that day?

I remember most . . .

_____

_____

_____

_____

_____

_____

_____

_____

_____

_____

Children, like animals, use all their senses to discover the world. —EUDORA WELTY

First Wings

I'll always remember the day my son forgot his lunch and I had to chase his school bus in my bunny slippers. I thought he'd never forgive me! "THOSE are so un-cool Mom," he pronounced, rolling his eyes in disbelief.

Your favorite teacher

_____

Your favorite food

_____

The name of your first school

_____

I'll always remember . . .

_____

_____

_____

_____

_____

_____

_____

The man in your life . . .

_____

_____

_____

_____

_____

_____

_____

_____

Boys Will Be Boys

"Mom! Mom! Look what we found!"

My eleven-year-old son, dressed like a pirate, came bounding into my kitchen one day with his best buddy close behind. "Look at all this neat stuff we dug up in the woods behind our house!" Then, with a ceremonious air, the boys unwrapped a rotting scrap of burlap and emptied its contents onto my freshly laundered table cloth.

From the rich black dirt all over my cutwork, I surmised that they had been digging in an old house dump. They went through their booty carefully, piece by piece, explaining the significance of rusty old scraps of metal, a dented teapot, and a cluster of broken dishes. Then my son held up a small heart-shaped chip of china. "I found this one for you, Mom!". . . The dirt was forgotten.

Things you liked to collect . . .

_____

_____

Your best adventures . . .

_____

_____

How you drove me nuts! . . .

_____

_____

Snips and Snails

Ever since he was small, my son has been passionate about getting dressed up in countless villainous costumes. One day he would be a soldier, the next day a knight. I hated the idea of my gentle son wielding swords and lopping off the heads of dragons! Rude machine gun sounds spewing from his innocent lips made my stomach turn tipsy turvy.

The other day we were out in the yard and he had an injured rabbit cradled between his long teenage fingers. As he crooned, softly consoling the frightened little creature, I couldn't help but remember my little warrior. I guess a loving spirit will always prevail.

The games you liked to play . . .

_____

_____

_____

_____

Things you thought were funny . . .

_____

_____

_____

_____

Our favorite pet . . .

_____

_____

_____

_____

Snips and snails and puppy dog's tails:
That's what little boys are made of.

—ANON

The great man is he who does not lose his child's heart.
—MENCIUS

Cooking Up Trouble

What is it about cooking with your children that can bring out the beast in everyone? We were baking peanut butter cookies. My four-year-old daughter was crying into a bowl of walnuts after hearing from her older brother that there would be a lot of starving squirrels that winter. He was out of control, banging a metal bowl with a spoon as he balanced it on his head pretending to be a hungry rodent. "This is supposed to be one of those precious moments?" I asked myself.

An hour later, as I sat munching on a cookie, I noticed my son outside placing a pile of nuts in the crook of a nearby tree with his sister.

My recipe for your favorite dish

_____

_____

_____

_____

_____

_____

_____

_____

_____

_____

_____

_____

S'mores

"Can we make S'mores?" asked Adam. The children sat toasting marshmallows over the glowing embers of a campfire. Adam was quite proud of the fact that he could toast his to a golden brown while Monique thought the burnt ones tasted like outdoors. Four-year-old Tyler scrunched up his nose and exclaimed, "That's a funny name!" "No it's not," answered Adam with a sticky grin. "When you eat one you always ask, 'can I have S'more?'"

RECIPE FOR "S'MORES"

Squish a toasted marshmallow and a chocolate bar between two graham crackers. Half the fun is tasting this delicious grahamwich and the other is licking the sticky goo off your fingers.

My Son, My Friend

I sometimes wish that I could go back in time for just one more three-year-old's peanut butter kiss. The years have flown by much too quickly. It seems like only yesterday he was climbing across the kitchen counter getting into mischief.

Today he looked down on me, gloating over how tall he'd grown. He kissed the top of my head and said, "Hey Mom, you've shrunk!" "What's that on your face?" I asked in return. "Is that peanut butter?"

Things you and I did together . . .

_____

_____

_____

_____

Teenagers are people who express a burning desi

What always came easily to you . . .

_____

_____

_____

_____

_____

My proudest moment . . .

_____

_____

_____

_____

_____

Your friends I've loved . . .

_____

_____

_____

_____

_____

_____

_____

_____

be different by dressing exactly alike. —ANON

The Best of Times

As a kaleidoscope of memories dance around in my heart, one day in particular always makes me smile. I can almost smell the salty air and feel the ocean breeze on my face as I remember that day my son caught his first fish. He was so proud! It was a simple thing. He just stood there holding that fish up for all to admire. It wasn't really planned. It was just one of those moments when I looked down at him and thought, "Wow, this is what it's all about!"

Do you remember . . .

_____

_____

_____

_____

_____

Make a memory with your children,
Spend some time to show you care,
Toys and trinkets can't replace those
Precious moments that you share.

—ELAINE HARDT

*The companions of our childhood always possess
a certain power over our minds which hardly
any later friend can obtain.*   —MARY SHELLY

Hanging On and Letting Go

One of the most difficult things about being a mother, I've found, has been knowing how much and when to let go of my son. It hasn't always been easy restraining myself from running to his rescue whenever he falls. I want to keep him under my protection yet I know that he needs to learn to use his own wings. When he was twelve years old he broke his back. After spending a year and a half in a body cast, he was sitting in the doctor's office one day asking how soon could he ride his mountain bike over jumps. The doctor looked at me and simply said, "It's better to mend a body than try to mend a broken spirit."

I guess it's all really about . . . faith.

Things you've struggled with . . .

_____

_____

_____

My greatest fear about letting go . . .

_____

_____

_____

Mothers don't really have premonitions. They have been over every possible eventuality so often—both good and ill—that whatever happens to you, they've rehearsed it. —PAM BROWN

Goals you've reached . . .

_____

_____

_____

Your inner strengths . . .

_____

_____

_____

To keep the body in good health is a duty . . . otherwise we shall not be able to keep our mind strong and clear.

—BUDDHA

All Grown Up

There never seems to be enough time to do all the things we'd like to do in a day. As mothers, we wear the hats of taxi drivers, diplomats, homework coaches, cooks, home maintenance supervisors, and financial specialists, not to mention caretakers and therapists. The list goes on and on! Before we realize it, the baby booties turn into construction boots. We look back and say, "If only" . . . but I guess what we should embrace is that we have done it all and said it all by just being there. We will forever be left with the need to say one more, "I love you more than life itself."

What I always meant to tell you . . .

_____

_____

_____

If I could replay just one day it would be the day . . .

_____

_____

_____

The image I'll always have of you will be . . .

_____

_____

_____

I'll Always Remember

My thoughts about our life together . . .

_____

_____

_____

_____

_____

_____

_____

_____

_____

_____

_____

_____

_____

_____

_____

_____

*For my friend Cindy and in loving
memory of her son, A.J.*

*It's not the years in your life but the life in your
years that counts.* —ADLAI STEVENSON

The Love of Your Life

I remember the first time I met the love of his life. She was somehow different from all of the previous young ladies he spent time with. They seemed to know each other's thoughts and needs without saying a word. Each was a beautiful reflection of the other. I felt a tug on my heart strings that day. I was both happy for him and envious of her.

My advice to you . . .

_____

_____

_____

_____

My dreams for you . . .

_____

_____

_____

_____

My promise to you . . . I'll always bite my tongue before interfering.

Your Wedding Day

On this, your wedding day, it is so difficult for me to put into words what I'm feeling. You've been my little boy forever; nothing will ever change that. Be happy my son!

Your wife's maiden name

_____

Where you were married

_____

_____

My deepest feelings on this day of days . . .

_____

_____

_____

_____

_____

The mother-child relationship is paradoxical . . . It requires the most intense love on the mother's side, yet this very love must help the child grow away from the mother, and to become fully independent.
    —ERICH FROMM

Private Thoughts

Here is my recipe for a happy life, the ingredients are simple. First, know yourself; you'll always know what to do next when difficulties arise. Second, live in the present. Savor every minute because time is what we have least of. Third, never stop learning. One of the surprises of growing older is that the mind doesn't. And finally, stay as wonderful as you are.

How you're like me and how we're different . . .

_____

_____

What you've taught me . . .

_____

_____

What I've learned from life. . .

_____

_____

I showed you the world through my eyes. Now you show it to me through yours. And so we learn. —PAM BROWN

You and I

It took me years to realize that the hardships laid in my path have been blessings in disguise. Through pain, I've learned patience. Through poverty, I understand true wealth. Through my handicaps, I've realized my strengths. Beauty born of character, and kindness learned by understanding fear, are the real gifts.

Being with you is like walking on a very clear morning— definitely the sensation of belonging there. —ANON

Once the children were in the house the air became more vivid and more heated; every object in the house grew more alive. —MARY GORDON

Our Family

We all gather once again—young and old, introvert and family clown, mischievous cousins, and emotional grandmothers whose eyes brim with pride. What would the day be without shared jokes, glorified achievements, and too much food? It's a time for the family to reaffirm itself and grow, to bond with newlyweds and precious new additions and to reminisce about loved ones lost. It's a day to laugh and hug and remember who we are.

Memories of our family life . . .

_____

_____

_____

_____

Our most important traditions . . .

_____

_____

_____

How we celebrate the holidays . . .

_____

_____

_____

The family—that dear octopus from whose tentacles we never quite escape, nor, in our inmost hearts, ever quite wish to.

—DODIE SMITH

That Special Person
Who Made a Difference in Your Life

It's often the small acts of kindness which end up being some of our greatest blessings. It took two seconds for the coolest counselor in a day camp to throw my son up on his shoulders. Two seconds to notice that it was open season on nine year olds.

RECIPE FOR GROWING BOYS

Take one boy, about seven pounds. Give to a family who loves him very much. Simmer together with laughter, patience, comfort and a deep sense of responsibility for about three years. Let season but watch carefully for signs of spoiling.

Mix one part firmness with two parts understanding. Add both at the same time, with mature wisdom. Let season. Then mix thoroughly the Golden Rule with some baseball, fishing trips, responsibilities, privacy, picnics, games and a cookie jar. Shake in some soap, toothpaste and a comb.

Now very slowly add some good books, some music, a football, a lawn mower and a savings account. Let season quite awhile. Then mix liberally with some dreams that make sense and some that don't; some for fun and some for growth. Stir in some good conversation about grades, honor, beliefs, love, patriotism, girls, cars and the World Series. Sprinkle with humor. . . . For extra interest, add a few roots such as integrity, fidelity, determination and gentleness. Mix with an interest in school activities, civic duty and his fellow man. Pour in some weekend jobs and a goal or two. Let season.

When you think he's ready, garnish with faith in tomorrow . . . and gaze with pride

—IRENE NOBLE

Someone you've admired

Your extended family

The one who baked you cookies

The one who cared for you whenever you were ill

Those who have made you feel good about yourself

Your best friends

Your favorite toy

The person who has taught you to care for others

The most important men in your life

The Most Beautiful Families A

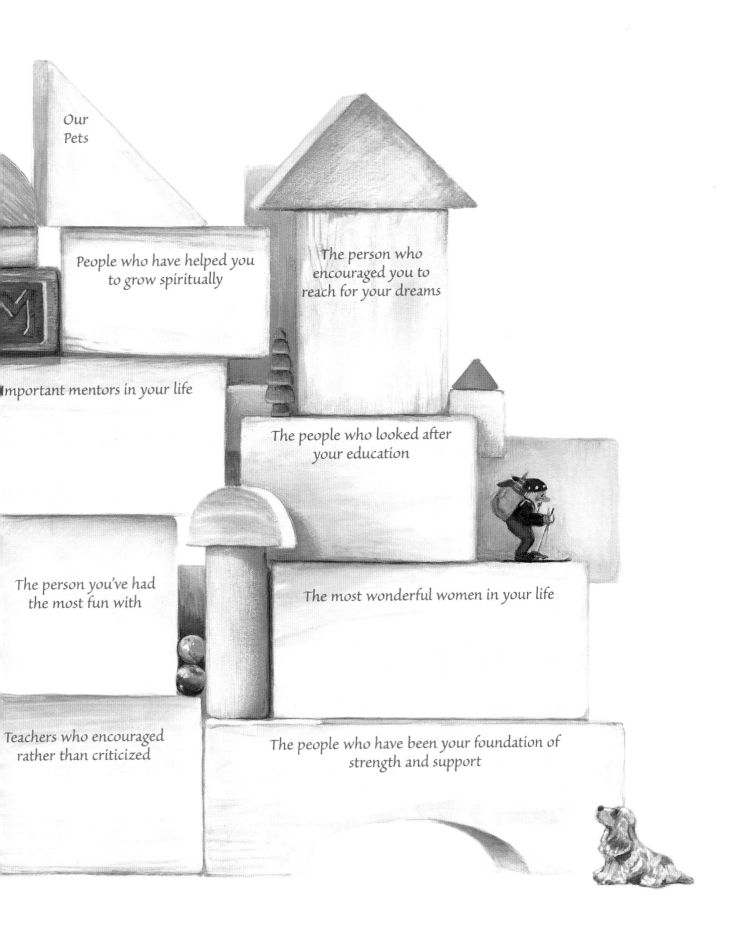

Our Pets

People who have helped you to grow spiritually

The person who encouraged you to reach for your dreams

Important mentors in your life

The people who looked after your education

The person you've had the most fun with

The most wonderful women in your life

Teachers who encouraged rather than criticized

The people who have been your foundation of strength and support

Built On a Foundation of Love

I hope my son looks back upon today
And sees a mother who had time to play.
Whether the work was done, or it was not;
Who realized chores are sometimes best forgot.
There will be years for cleaning house and cooking,
But little boys grow up when we're not looking.

—BARBARA OVERTON CHRISTIE

The Circle Game

Yesterday a child came out to wonder
Caught a dragonfly inside a jar
Fearful when the sky was full of thunder
And tearful at the falling of a star
Then the child moved ten times round the seasons
Skated over ten clear frozen streams
Words like when you're older, must appease him

And promises of someday make his dreams

And the seasons they go round and round
And the painted ponies go up and down
We're captive on the carousel of time
We can't return we can only look behind
From where we came
And go round and round and round
In the circle game

Sixteen springs and sixteen summers gone now
Cartwheels turn to car wheels thru the town
And they tell him, TAKE your time, it won't be long now
Till you drag your feet to slow the circles down

And the seasons they go round and round
And the painted ponies go up and down
We're captive on the carousel of time
We can't return we can only look behind
From where we came
And go round and round and round